Aboriginal and Torres Strait Islander people should be aware that this
book contains images and names of deceased persons.

A Lothian Children's Book

Published in Australia and New Zealand in 2021
by Hachette Australia

Level 17, 207 Kent Street, Sydney NSW 2000

www.hachettechildrens.com.au

10 9 8 7 6 5 4 3 2 1

 A catalogue record for this
book is available from the
National Library of Australia

ISBN 978 0 7344 1983 5 (hardback)

Cover and internal design by Christabella Designs

Printed in China by Toppan Leefung Printing Limited

HEROES, REBELS

····· AND ·····
INNOVATORS

INSPIRING ABORIGINAL AND TORRES STRAIT ISLANDER PEOPLE FROM HISTORY

····························

KAREN WYLD AND
JAELYN BIUMAIWAI

LOTHIAN
Children's Books

Introduction

Within these pages are seven stories about Aboriginal and Torres Strait Islander people from the past. Be inspired by:

- **Patyegarang**, a Darug woman, taught an officer of the First Fleet how to communicate with Aboriginal people in Sydney Cove.

- **Bungaree**, a Darug man, circumnavigated Australia with Matthew Flinders.

- Legendary resistance fighter of the Tommeginne people, **Tarenorerer** dreamed of freedom.

- Wiradjuri men **Yarri** and **Jacky Jacky** rescued dozens of settlers from freezing flood waters.

- Torres Strait Islander **Mohara Wacando-Lifu** was the first Indigenous woman awarded the Royal Humane Society's Gold Medal for bravery.

- Ngarrindjeri inventor and author **David Unaipon**'s image features on the $50 note.

- **Fanny Balbuk Yooreel**, a Whadjuk woman, tried to teach settlers how to care for the environment.

Karen Wyld, a writer of Martu descent, and Jaelyn Biumaiwai, an illustrator of Mununjali and Fijian descent, combine their interests and skills to bring you these real-life stories of Aboriginal and Torres Strait Islander people who readers of all ages should know about.

British invasion and settlement caused upheaval for Aboriginal and Torres Strait Islander peoples, but the heroes, rebels and innovators featured in this book still held on to their dreams. What dream will you turn into reality?

Contents

Patyegarang

· UNDER THE LIGHT OF YAN·NĂ·DAH ·

In the darkness, they watch the stranger.

He looks like the others who arrived by sea but he's also different.

This one lives in a shelter of cloth and gazes at stars as if he knows their names.

A young woman steps out from the shadows and walks towards the fire.

He offers food. She takes a bite. It tastes strange.

'William,' he says, tapping his chest. 'William Dawes.'

'Will yim,' she repeats. 'Pa te ga rang'

At the sound of children laughing in the shadows, Patyegarang leaves.

She appears the next night, when he is watching the sky.

William smiles at Patyegarang, and turns back towards the stars.

Patyegarang tells him stories of Yan-nă-dah (the moon).

William tells her of the comet he'd travelled so far to see.

'What is this place called?' asks William.

'Tar-ra,' says Patyegarang, warming her hands over the campfire.

She takes his hand, 'Putuwá' (touch someone's fingers with your warmed hand).

William begs Patyegarang to teach him more.

Patyegarang teaches him Darug – her language.

William shows her how to read and write in English – his language.

Putting down his telescope, William sees stars through Patyegarang's stories.

Together, William and Patyegarang make the first books featuring Aboriginal languages.

Lieutenant William Dawes is being sent back to England.

William takes a last look at the place he'd wanted to call home.

As the ship disappears, Patyegarang whispers, 'Whalloo?' (Where are you going?)

Then she walks away from Tar-ra (Dawes Point).

In 1791, Patyegarang, a young Darug woman, met Lieutenant William Dawes. William was an officer in the Royal Marines who had travelled from England with the First Fleet in 1788. He'd been instructed to set up an observatory and watch for an expected comet.

Patyegarang acted as a liaison between local Aboriginal people and the British at Sydney Cove.

William was interested in sciences, such as botany and astronomy, and recorded everything in his notebooks. William wanted to communicate with local Aboriginal people, so Patyegarang taught him words from local dialects. And William taught her how to read and write English.

Before the British arrived, there were over 250 distinct Aboriginal languages and hundreds more dialects. Patyegarang and Dawes wrote the first list of Aboriginal words. William's forgotten notebooks were rediscovered in 1972 and helped preserve Darug language.

A few months after Patyegarang and William met, Governor Arthur Phillip ordered him to return to England. William later became an anti-slavery campaigner. There is no record of what happened to Patyegarang.

Bungaree

· NAUTICAL ADVENTURER ·

Bungaree, soon to be King, leads his people to the coast.

Some follow reluctantly, yearning for their campsites.

Not Bungaree. He struts into Sydney, Cora Gooseberry by his side.

Bungaree can feel change in the air, and he wants to be a part of it.

The crowd laugh loudly as Bungaree mimics the Governor.

Grinning, Bungaree tugs at his hand-me-down military coat.

Then he struts like a rooster, entertaining all who gather.

They may laugh but Bungaree is no one's fool.

Bungaree is offered a job on a ship and sails south, far from land.

Then Matthew Flinders invites Bungaree to sail with him, all around Australia.

In daylight, Flinders draws maps. At night, he listens to Bungaree's stories.

Bungaree spears fish, offering tasty morsels to Flinders' cat, Trim.

Bungaree travels to the west coast, with Phillip Parker King.

Their ship is beached for repairs but Bungaree keeps the crew safe.

'You eat that plant. Not that one,' he tells them.

Mermaid, the ship, returns them safely to Sydney.

There, Governor Macquarie gives Bungaree the title King of Broken Bay.

Macquarie gifts him a bronze kingplate and a farm.

King Bungaree and Queen Cora move to the country, to eat peaches.

Having sailed around Australia, Bungaree soon finds farming boring.

He returns to Sydney, to greet ships as they arrive in the Cove.

Bungaree becomes sick. Long-time sick; then gone.

Many remember the clown, too few remember the wise man.

Trim has many statues. Where is Bungaree's statue?

Bungaree, a Darug man, and his wife Cora Gooseberry were fascinated by the British colony that became Sydney in the 1790s. Quickly learning English, and with a keen sense of humour, Bungaree became popular with the British. He treasured the old military coats and tricorn hat they gave him.

Bungaree was fascinated with boats. He did short trips before sailing with Matthew Flinders on HMS *Investigator* in 1802, to map the coast of Australia.

Flinders was fond of his cat, Trim, who always sailed with him. Flinders recorded in his journal how kind Bungaree was to Trim.

Bungaree sailed with Phillip Parker King to the west coast on HMS *Mermaid*. Bungaree taught the crew about fishing and which plants to eat.

In Sydney, Governor Macquarie gave Bungaree a breastplate with *King of Broken Bay* on it, and granted him a farm.

Bungaree died in 1830. Despite Bungaree's reputation as a diplomat and explorer, there are no monuments to honour him.

Tarenorerer

◦ FREEDOM FIGHTER ◦

They took Tarenorerer from her mother's arms.

Sold her to white men, who took her to another island.

These sealers ordered her to work but she refused to listen.

They punished her, but Tarenorerer still dreamed of freedom.

Tarenorerer watched. She saw how those men used rifles.

Tarenorerer listened. She learnt their language.

Tarenorerer remembered. She missed her family.

Tarenorerer waited. She was ready for her moment to escape.

Returning home, Tarenorerer was saddened by the destruction.

She still burnt with anger, remembering how the sealers treated her.

Tarenorerer wanted vengeance for her people. For her Country.

So she showed her brothers and sisters how to fight the settlers.

Tarenorerer bravely led the resistance fighters in their battle for freedom.

From the top of hills she would taunt the settlers: *fight me, luta tawin.*

The settlers were afraid, not knowing where the Black Amazon would next strike.

Tarenorerer's army grew bigger and stronger, but she was not invincible.

Captured by sealers again, Tarenorerer said her name was Mary Anne.

They made her hunt seals on Hunter Island and catch mutton birds on Bird Island.

They took Tarenorerer to another island, where Whiskey the dog recognised her.

Alerted by the barking, people noticed the legendary freedom fighter.

Worried she would reassemble her army, they imprisoned Tarenorerer.

Dreaming of her people living free on Country, Tarenorerer died in captivity.

A lone bird flew to the north coast, carrying Tarenorerer's dream.

To this day, people still speak of Tarenorerer – the freedom fighter.

Tarenorerer, also known as Walyer, was born in about 1800 on the north coast of Tasmania, on Tommeginne Country.

When she was a teenager, Tarenorerer was kidnapped by sealers (white men who hunted seals). Forcing Aboriginal people to be unpaid workers was common in those days.

Years later, she escaped and returned home. Tarenorerer was dismayed by the harm settlers had caused and was determined to stop the luta tawin (white men).

In 1828, with her brothers Linnetower and Line-ne-like-kayver, two sisters, and other Aboriginal people, Tarenorerer led armed attacks against the settlers. Some settlers called Tarenorerer the Amazon of Van Diemen's Land (the name first given to Tasmania by white settlers), for her fearless combat skills.

Captured by settlers, Tarenorerer was forced to gather food for them. After she was recognised by her dog Whiskey, British authorities locked up Tarenorerer. She died of influenza shortly afterwards, in 1831.

Tarenorerer is remembered as a daring fighter for her people's freedom.

Yarri and Jacky Jacky

· HEROES OF GUNDAGAI ·

They told them not to build there, so close to the Murrumbidgee River.

Wiradjuri warned them – plenty water overflows there.

They showed them safer places to build their houses and businesses.

The settlers refused to listen, and built a town called Gundagai.

Year after year, rains fell and the river rose, creeping towards their doors.

This isn't too bad, the settlers remarked.

After two people died in a flood, the settlers became concerned.

A few years later, a most fearsome storm arrived.

The river rose, breaking its bank, rushing towards Gundagai.

In the moonlight, the raging water engulfed the town.

Sheep, horses, people. All struggled in the freezing cold waters.

Buildings were swept away. Plenty water took everything.

The sound of crashing buildings finally stopped.

People clung to tree-tops, water lapping at their feet.

Cries for help continued for days, becoming fainter and fainter.

Scar trees kept some safe, and called to the canoes made from their bark.

Yarri and Jacky Jacky rowed those bark canoes for three days.

As heavy rain fell, Long Jimmy, Tommy Davis and others helped.

A few at a time, they carried people to safety in the small canoes.

Wiradjuri fought off exhaustion, as they answered cries for help.

Afterwards, the settlers listened. They rebuilt the town on higher ground.

Yarri, Jacky Jacky and Tommy Davis were given shiny necklaces.

Not Long Jimmy; those cold flood waters had made him too sick.

The Wiradjuri heroes of Gundagai are long gone, but will never be forgotten.

The original township of Gundagai in New South Wales was built on the Murrumbidgee flood plains. Wiradjuri (local Aboriginal people) had warned the settlers not to build there, but they were ignored.

In June 1852, more than seventy people died when the river flooded. Many were swept away in the water, while others clung to roofs and tree-tops for days.

Wiradjuri rescued townsfolk, using bark canoes that could only carry a few at a time. Trees that canoes have been cut from are called scar trees.

Yarri rescued forty-nine people and Jacky Jacky rescued twenty. Long Jimmy, Tommy Davis and other Wiradjuri helped. Afterwards, Long Jimmy died from exposure to the cold waters.

Many years later, Yarri, Jacky Jacky and Tommy Davis were honoured with bronze breastplates. A statue depicting the Wiradjuri heroes stands in the newer township of Gundagai.

Mohara Wacando-Lifu

· ESCAPE FROM MAHINA ·

One hundred boats toss on the waves. To be shattered – sinking.

Fish lie stunned in trees, while sharks take their final breath on cliff-tops.

Trees take flight, like birds on the wind, only to crash to the ground.

Mahina stamps her place in history: the greatest of all tropical cyclones.

A streak of lightning exposes Mahina's ferocious eye.

Winds lash the pearling boats that sought shelter in the bays.

Onboard the *Silvery Wave*, newlyweds Mohara and William watch in fear.

Mahina rages on, breaking ships' masts and sending others to the sea floor.

Mohara treads water as she watches the boat sink.

Separated from her husband, her tears mix with the salty sea.

Determined to survive, Mohara swims towards the distant shore.

Four kilometres of raging sea and biting winds lie before her.

With the stamina of a young dugong, Mohara swims on.

She comes across two sailors, floundering in the sea.

Mohara knows these Europeans cannot out-swim a cyclone.

'I will show you the way,' says Mohara.

Exhausted, the men cling to Mohara's back.

Every muscle aching, she keeps the shore in sight.

The cyclone's tail lashes at those struggling in the water.

Seven hours later, all three crawl onto land.

The settlers show Mohara their appreciation with a gold medal for bravery.

Mohara returns to Erub, her island home, to raise a family with her husband.

Many decades later, Mohara is still remembered as a hero.

A memorial of shell and coral adorns her grave on Waiben.

In 1899, tropical cyclone Mahina caused chaos in the Torres Strait and Bathurst Bay in Far North Queensland.

Over 300 people died, which is the biggest loss of life by a cyclone ever recorded in written Australian history. When the eye of the cyclone hit on 5 March, most of the eight schooners and eighty luggers of a pearling fleet were destroyed.

The crews were from the Torres Strait Islands, New Guinea, Malaysia, the Pacific Islands, Japan and elsewhere.

William Wacando-Lifu, from Lifou Island in the South Pacific, and Mohara (nee Newi), from the Torres Strait were working on the vessel *Silvery Wave* when the cyclone hit.

When Mohara was swimming towards the shore she saw two sailors struggling. They clung to Mohara's back as she swam to safety.

Mohara, of Torres Strait Islander, Nuie Islander and Papua New Guinea heritage, was the first Indigenous woman awarded the Royal Humane Society's Gold Medal for bravery. There is a memorial for Mohara on Waiben (Thursday Island).

David Unaipon

· PERPETUAL KNOWLEDGE ·

David Unaipon, son of Nymbulda and James Ngunaitponi.

Cobbler, preacher, writer, inventor, father.

Mission-born, but boundless mind.

Proud Ngarrindjeri korni (man).

David was always thinking, reading, learning, doing.

Watching sedge grass sway in the breeze, he pondered perpetual motion.

As a lone kungari (black swan) flew over the water, he thought of gravity.

Gazing at the stars, David wondered how long it would take to reach the moon.

In the woolsheds, David imagined an easier way to shear sheep.

He turned imagination into pictures, which became improved shears.

Watching a boomerang fly, David imagined a flying machine.

He had no money to build that machine, but knew it would be real one day.

David wanted more people to know about the world's oldest knowledges.

He put Ngarrindjeri stories on paper, becoming the first Aboriginal author.

He wrote about Indigenous sciences, and gave talks in universities.

David spoke about Ngarrindjeri, and their dreams of equality and rights.

So he talked to people, to plan the way forward.

He met with government, suggesting ways of working together.

He spoke to the kringkari (white men), to help them open their minds.

Some people looked down on him but no one could stop David Unaipon.

Up until his last day, the Black Da Vinci dared to dream big.

He never stopped dreaming of perpetual motion becoming a reality.

He never stopped hoping that one day all people would be free to dream.

In honour of a legendary man, David's image is on the fifty-dollar note.

Ngarrindjeri innovator David Unaipon was born on Point McLeay Mission (Raukkan) in South Australia, in 1872. David was one of Nymbulda and James Ngunaitponi's nine children. Their family name was changed to Unaipon.

Like his father, David Unaipon was a preacher. As a young man he worked as a bootmaker, storeman and bookkeeper. Acknowledging David's intelligence and vision, some people called him the Black Da Vinci.

David designed over nineteen inventions, but couldn't get funding to build them. Mechanical devices he invented include a centrifugal motor, multi-radial wheel and an improved sheep-shearing handpiece. His other ideas were lasers, helicopters and anti-gravitational devices.

An Aboriginal rights advocate, he wrote fiction, poetry, non-fiction and newspaper articles. David was the first Aboriginal writer to have a book published.

David was still envisioning a perpetual motion device (a machine that works indefinitely without an energy source) when he died in 1967 at the age of 94. His image features on the Australian fifty-dollar note.

Fanny Balbuk Yooreel

· THE WOMAN WHO WALKED THROUGH WALLS ·

The land and waters of her ancestors nourished Fanny Balbuk Yooreel.

Zamia fruit, honey and berries for sweetness.

Duck eggs, turtles and crayfish from the wetland.

On her way home, a chorus of frogs wished her goodnight.

More and more colonisers arrived – and stayed.

Streets and railroad tracks now crisscrossed Noongar Country.

Sheep moved through the land like a plague of locust.

Houses popped up everywhere. Colonisers had become settlers.

Some settlers fondly remembered the spirited Aboriginal girl.

The one who had played with the settlers' children.

Now she stormed through town, reminding them whose land they stood on.

None of them were children anymore. Playtime was over.

Fanny Balbuk Yooreel, Whadjuk yorga, became a resistance fighter.

If a fence was built between her and the swamp, she'd climb over it.

She'd open settlers' front doors, only to walk straight through and out the back doors.

At the gates of Government House, she'd loudly voice her concerns.

A formidable environmental protector, she kept resisting.

She knew that settlers and sheep had to tread more carefully.

Turning their backs on Fanny Balbuk, settlers didn't listen to the warnings.

She shook her head. *Country is everything; why can't they understand?*

Too weary to get out of bed, she thought of the destruction she'd witnessed.

She'd lost her taste for settler food, and dreamed of nourishing bushtucker.

Her husband Doolby offered to go hunting for her.

Fanny Balbuk Yooreel shook her head; she'd lost her appetite for life.

Fanny Balbuk Yooreel, a Whadjuk yorga (woman), was a resistance fighter who tried to teach white people how to care for the environment.

Born on Noongar Country in about 1840, she had connections on both sides of Derbarl Yerrigan (Swan River, Perth). She was taught to care for Country and community. Like her grandfather, Mooro leader Yellagonga, Fanny Balbuk took this responsibility seriously.

As a child, she made friends with the settlers' children. This may have been why they didn't always call the police when, as an adult, she loudly protested against colonisation and destruction of the environment.

There was much to protest. It upset her that Government House was built on the site where Moojurngul, her grandmother, had been buried. Fanny Balbuk would yell through the gates, reminding those inside of what they'd done.

In 1907, at about 67 years of age, Fanny Balbuk Yooreel died with her husband Doolby by her side.

AUTHOR'S ACKNOWLEDGEMENTS

I acknowledge that I live on unceded Kaurna Country. I pay my respects to Kaurna Elders, and Elders across the continent; past and present.

Much gratitude to Hachette for publishing my first book for children. Particularly Suzanne O'Sullivan, who had the concept for an illustrated book that highlighted Aboriginal and Torres Strait Islander peoples' achievements and resistance during early colonisation eras. Suzanne is no longer with Hachette, so thank you Karen Ward and Jeanmarie Morosin for completing this project. And thank you Jaelyn Biumaiwai, for bringing these stories to life through your unique artwork.

One of the many people who inspired me as I wrote this book is Kerry Klimm, a strong voice for improving the quality of books about Aboriginal and Torres Strait Islander peoples within schools and libraries. Thank you, sis.

And I am grateful for the time and advice given to me by descendants and communities of the Aboriginal and Torres Strait Islander people featured in this book.

ILLUSTRATOR'S ACKNOWLEDGEMENTS

I acknowledge that I live and create on Kombumerri land, and pay my respects to Elders past and present.

A big thank you to Suzanne O'Sullivan for approaching me and giving me the opportunity to illustrate my first book, for guiding me along the way and making my first book illustrating experience less intimidating. Thank you to Karen Wyld for her extensive research and words, to create this book and have it available for readers to learn more about Aboriginal and Torres Strait Islander peoples and history. Thank you to Karen Ward and Jeanmarie Morosin from Hachette, for your help along the way. Another thank you to Emma Kerslake for her guidance in the early stages of this journey.

AUTHOR'S NOTE

The process to ensure the content was respectful and accurate was time-consuming and often challenging. This was necessary to ensure the book was culturally appropriate and honoured peoples' ancestors. In addition to engaging with communities and organisations, I took care with the resources I used. Words, and even stories, were removed because I was unable to engage with the right people or was not satisfied with the accuracy of the archival material. As a writer of Martu descent, I accept that I am accountable for any inaccuracies or disrespect, even if unintentional.

Please note that the spelling of First Nations words in this book may differ from what is used elsewhere. While care was taken to ensure accuracy, some words may not use the current or future preferred spelling.

I encourage readers of all ages to learn more about Aboriginal and Torres Strait Islander peoples, languages and histories. Always use reputable resources, such as Aboriginal and Torres Strait Islander authored books and websites.

There are Teachers' Notes on the Hachette website that will assist in further discussion, research and learning. These will include some of the resources used to develop this book.

www.hachettechildrens.com.au